Born on the cusp of Sagittarius and Capricorn in 1942, Ann Jones, a psychic consultant, has for the past 20 years, been involved in many aspects of spiritual development. She lives and practises in the Midlands where she has an enormous following. Since the publication of her first book *Ann Jones A Way of Life*, she has been in even greater demand for private consultations, public meetings and as a frequent contributor to local radio station programmes.

Also by Ann Jones
ANN JONES A WAY OF LIFE
published by EAJ publications

Other booklets by Ann Jones and from the same publisher
CRYSTAL MAGIC - Reading the Crystal Ball
GHOSTS
GHOSTS 2
TAROT - A Guide to Tarot

ANN JONES
THOUGHTS ON THE WAY

EAJ Publications

ANN JONES THOUGHTS ON THE WAY
First published in 1994 by
EAJ PUBLICATIONS
18 Chapel Street, Astwood Bank,
Redditch, Worcestershire, B96 6DA.

Copyright © 1994 Ann Jones

ISBN 0 9519210 1 0

No part of this book may be reproduced in any form
without the publisher's prior consent in writing.

Design & Artwork by MOSS DESIGN

*To Whom I Have Known Before
and Will Know Again.*

In memory of my Mother and Father,
and dear friends Hazel and Muriel.

CONTENTS

Introduction *8*

1 The Paranormal *9*

2 Life After Death *12*

3 Astral Levels and Reincarnation *20*

4 Spirit Guides *24*

5 Dreams *27*

6 Meditation *30*

7 Hidden Dangers *32*

8 Further Ghost Hunting *36*

9 Planet Earth *48*

Conclusion *54*

Glossary *55*

INTRODUCTION

Since my first book was published two years ago, the response from readers has been overwhelming. I'm pleased to say that it has stimulated a great deal of interest, provoked much thought and debate, but above all appears to have given comfort, security and encouragement to those embarking on development of their awareness.

Before writing this second book, I asked my readers what, as a result of absorbing my first, they would wish a second to contain, and which they would find both interesting and necessary to lead one stage further along the spiritual pathway.

The consensus was for a similar format but to include a more detailed focus on *Life After Death*, *The Astral Levels* and the role of *Spirit Guides*.

It was obvious that most readers enjoy hearing about spirit encounters, and so in this book I have enlarged the chapter that describes my ghostly experiences. I have also included a chapter relating some of my other adventures which emphasises the danger of meddling with the unknown. My readers will I'm sure take this point very seriously!

As requested I have introduced, quite briefly, the subject of *meditation*.

Earth matters concern people more and more, so finally I have grouped together some brief outlines of related matters, which I hope the reader will find both informative and thought provoking.

I'm sure many readers will elect to read the book straight through, but I have assumed that it will also be a book to return to for reference, and in that case the reader may only dip into certain chapters. Therefore to allow for this, certain information has been duplicated in a different form.

I hope you will find this book as helpful and as supportive as my first. Please let me know.

chapter 1
THE PARANORMAL

What is the paranormal? Many books have been written on this subject over a period of time and today people are searching through much of this literature to try to understand the meaning of the word and what it is all about. I prefer to use the words *extended normality*, because many things which people considered abnormal as a result of earlier teaching and upbringing, are now seen to be acceptable and therefore *normal*.

Words like astrology, spiritualism, earth energies, crop circles and UFOs are all referred to as being paranormal, and yet we are beginning to realise that there is nothing abnormal in any of these matters. People are beginning to remove the constraints that have been put on their minds. In these troubled times people are seeking a light at the end of a tunnel and in so doing are finding themselves on a pathway to the inner truth. What one must realise is that all spiritual knowledge is within, and I feel we must search and explore many pathways to understand the laws and mysteries of existence which will slowly make us aware of the divine will of God.

Because of my work, misguided people have often accused me of being involved with the occult, as though this was an evil thing. However the original meaning of the word should be understood, rather than what it has come to mean, before making such judgements. The word occult comes from the Latin word *occultis* which translated means *hidden knowledge and wisdom*.

Occultism is a very comprehensive system of thought, and those who are interested in the practical development of spiritual powers latent in every human being, will at some point touch on occultism. It simply covers all the hidden things of nature and those hidden deeply within the human psyche. Radio, television and the telephone have all harnessed natural hidden energies in a way which would have been ridiculed in an earlier age. If our minds are opened what more is there to be discovered for the greater good of mankind?

Unlike science and many religions, *occultism* does not ignore spiritual and psychic experience. It makes use of many areas which bring us into relationships with greater worlds and the cosmic life force. We can look to the Bible for many words and phrases of wisdom and knowledge. Many of us have read the Bible and learnt from church doctrines how we should interpret what is written, but as we all know, with an open mind many different interpretations are possible. For instance what could be made of the saying in the early part of the Bible which states: *And the sons of God looked upon the daughters of man and saw they were fair.*

Could it indicate that a more evolved and enlightened race, perhaps from another solar system, took for themselves the daughters of men as wives, thus providing for us inner occult knowledge and wisdom to be handed down through genes for many centuries, so that when the time is right the knowledge can be released? Is the age of Aquarius the time? Is this the reason why so many people are turning to what in the past would have been referred to in a derogatory way as the occult?

There are many ways of thinking along these same lines, for instance when people think they receive divine guidance they could be tapping into the genes of their ancestors who have come from another dimension. All this may seem an extreme way of thinking, but the idea should be carefully considered before it is dismissed out of hand. The Bible holds many secrets and perhaps the *sons of God* were spiritual instructors of the world; there is no doubt that each race has at some time produced its own Masters to teach enlightenment when the time was right. Have we really understood the Bible teachings, have the churches always got their interpretations correct, or do we have a book of great knowledge with even more truths to unfold? We have always been taught that the Bible is one of the greatest books ever written and I do not believe this can be disputed.

In this material world everyone is trying to find some happiness, but most of our suffering is caused by our own ignorance. We are quick to blame others for our problems, and yet often without realising it we constantly cause suffering for others. Take the animal kingdom for example; every day millions of animals all over the world are being slaughtered, often very inhumanely, and those whose response to this is that they are only animals, are very misguided indeed. Animals are highly evolved beings especially creatures such as whales and dolphins, who it is thought are far more spiritually evolved than humans. Animals do feel pain and know suffering; even by buying meat you are encouraging this destruction of the animal kingdom. What gives us this right to inflict so much suffering on others and then complain about our own problems and afflictions. Maybe if we spent more time where possible reducing the suffering in this world, our own lives could be turned around and our problems eased.

Many people believe that spiritual enlightenment will be given by belonging to various religions and sects. They think by attending churches, putting money in collecting bowls or paying contributions, they will have the spiritual work done for them. All spiritual knowledge is for everyone to find for themselves and we have to go within ourselves to find it. We have to work at it personally and not expect others to provide us with the answers or to tell us the way. Spiritual enlightenment is a personal quest; we need guidance, but we must do the work.

You will find a lot of the esoteric teachings by the Masters tell us exactly this. We have to find the Wisdom for ourselves, and only then will we find the whole truth. We must remove the blinkers from our spiritual eyes and be prepared to uncover the Ancient Wisdom which is all around us in signs and symbols and esoteric knowledge.

chapter 2
LIFE AFTER DEATH

Does the spirit live after death? There is no doubt life goes on, but what proof is there of this? People receive proof in different ways; I have received proof of the next world many times, as do people attending Spiritualist Church meetings almost every night of the week. However we should look carefully at this evidence and the way we receive it.

Are names and details of the person who has died, given to us through a medium, proof? Although a medium myself, I would say not always, for the power of the mind is great and can sometimes influence a medium working from the platform; it is possible that the deep thoughts and desires of members of the audience are intercepted telepathically by the medium. This is not communication with the dead but telepathic communication with the mind of the living. We must be aware of this possibility, but that is not to dismiss the very strong survival evidence of the spirit given through clairvoyants and mediums.

I feel that some of the best evidence comes when the information given is not instantly recognised, and the receiver has to research and question others to find the accuracy of the message. This certainly removes any possibility of thought transference if the receiver at that time is unaware of the truth of the message.

Does a message about the future prove evidence of survival of the spirit? Again I think not because many mediums have this amazing ability to tune into the Akashic Records (historical records held on the astral plane, of all world events, past, present and future, and personal experiences of all thoughts and deeds which have taken place on the earth). The ability to tune into this vibration and access facts which will benefit not only individuals but sometimes the whole of humanity, is a wonderful gift, but we must realise that this information is not coming from spirit and therefore does not prove survival. It certainly proves the existence of another plane with workings beyond our comprehension, but in this chapter we are aiming to establish that our spirits will live on after death.

So whereas I would say that indicating a house move is not necessarily spirit communication, giving the enquirer details about a personal possession, possibly one passed down to them, or giving details of favourite flowers for example, certainly is. Personal evidence of this kind indicates an emotional link, an understanding between people built up during a lifetime and continuing beyond the grave. Such relationships could well have been built up with others connected with the enquirer, and that is when research within the family throws up amazing evidence of survival of the spirit.

In the past there have been incredible examples of mediumship, and I regret that much of this is now lost. Interest has waned with the onset of television; too many of us are now satisfied by just sitting and staring at the box, and having our minds occupied by whatever the media choose to inflict on us. We really should regain the art of thinking for ourselves, keeping our minds open to all possibilities, asking questions and constantly investigating.

Let me now relate experiences of other people which I hope will prove beyond a doubt the survival of the spirit.

The lady to whom this story relates is still alive and I correspond with her regularly, although I have only met her once.

Some years ago I was working at a psychic fair in Swindon and staying over night in a hotel. Towards the middle of Saturday afternoon, an older lady came into the fair and asked me to give her a reading. I was having some refreshment at the time, so I moved to my table and started to take up the cards. As I did this she took hold of my hand and said 'No, just talk to me'. I was a little surprised, but as I looked at her, the messages came.

I brought her husband through, and then other relatives she could recognise; they gave the type of personal information I mentioned earlier.

Still holding my hand, she asked me if I would have tea with her in the hotel. I agreed and she told me the most remarkable story. During the war she and her husband owned a corner shop. Her husband was called up for service, and she was left to bring up her three year old daughter as well as running the shop on her own.

She told me that she had always believed in life after death; this belief helped her considerably, and enabled her to survive when the news came that her husband had been killed in battle. She had sensed once that he had come to her, but she did not speak about this to anyone.

She had heard that one of the houses in the village held meetings which were rumoured to be about making contact with spirits. This sort of activity was frowned upon at that time and all such activities had to be held behind closed doors. One day the owner of this house came into the shop saying that she had been asked to invite her to a meeting, and that if she came the cost would be two pounds. This was a lot of money in those days and although she was tempted, she needed new shoes and also someone would need to look after her daughter while the meeting took place.

There was a gentleman who helped her with the heavy shop work, and she told him about the lady's invitation. He told her that she should go, and although part of her wanted to, the other half was afraid, and she really did need the shoes which she had saved so hard for. The evening came and she was still undecided. Her friend repeated his instinctive feeling that she should go, and he reassured her that he would look after the little girl and the shop. With great trepidation the lady agreed to go.

She was at the top of the long path approaching the cottage when suddenly the door opened and the owner emerged.

'We are expecting you', she said 'come on in, you are most welcome'.

Cynically she thought to herself 'Yes I bet I am or rather my two pounds is'.

She was not at all sure what to expect and found herself in a room with four other people. In the corner of the room was a black box with some curtains around it. The window curtains in the room were drawn and a small red light glowed in the corner. After a while a lady walked into the room, she did not speak to anyone but walked straight into the box.

Suddenly, my new found friend explained to me, she could see white stuff as she called it, knowing later that it was ectoplasm, emerging from the box, and a figure appeared to build up from it. As the figure took shape it was undeniably the figure of my story teller's husband. She could not believe what she was seeing or hearing when her husband actually spoke to her, held her and even danced around with her. After his appearance, slowly in turn, someone appeared for each individual there.

She had watched in amazement and kept pinching herself to make sure it was real and not a dream. Eventually the evening was over, the Medium did not speak to them; she looked weary and immediately retired to another room. When my friend started to walk home the Medium was just getting into a taxi and she called out asking whether she would like a lift home. My friend was very grateful because she had at least a mile to walk home in the dark. As the taxi dropped her off at the shop, the Medium took her hand and said 'Do not worry about the shoes, you will have them'.

Again she was shocked; how could anyone else possibly know about the shoes? She thanked the Medium and went into the shop. The gentleman who was looking after her daughter could see by her face that she had not been disappointed. She was full of enthusiasm, but she could tell that he did not really believe her story.

He told her that while she had been away someone had called to pay a bill. On opening the envelope she could not believe her eyes, for it was payment of a bill that she had written off as a bad debt some months ago. The amount of the bill, just two pounds! The Medium was right; she would have her shoes after all. She went to bed, her mind full of what had happened that evening, and the memory of being together again with her beloved husband was all she could have asked for.

The next day a customer came in to the shop, saying that she was on her way to the next town to take some shoes back for her daughter. They had been bought in a sale and were the wrong size. My friend asked what size they were and what they were like. When she opened the package, the shoes were not only her size but the colour and style she wanted.

She offered to buy them, to the great delight of her customer, who was being saved a journey and her bus fare into the next town. When she enquired the price she was told that they were one pound, because they were half price in the sale. Not only had she been able to afford her shoes, they had been brought to her doorstep.

The Medium concerned was the great Helen Duncan, who was many times called a fraud. However those who said so had never met my friend, for she had her proof, and what amazing proof it turned out to be.

This lady who I only once met at a psychic fair became a regular correspondent and dear friend; she wrote this story down for me in case I ever forgot the details, but I will never forget her telling it to me on that day in a hotel in Swindon. Nor do I have any doubts about the truth of her story. She became a committed spiritualist after this experience, but she never had evidence again quite like that experienced during the war years.

I have met many people over the years who have helped me travel the pathway, some I have kept in touch with and others have lost contact.

On the day of writing this chapter I received a telephone call from a lady who knew of my reputation. She asked me to put her mind at rest by answering a question that had been bothering her. She wanted to know whether people who had died could contact the living over the telephone. My immediate reply was 'Yes of course'.

She then proceeded to tell me the following story; her husband, who is in business, spends Monday to Friday in a flat near to his place of work. During the last three days his answer phone had recorded at least 75 calls, on which no one had spoken and the handset had been immediately replaced. On Friday evening as he was getting ready to return home for the weekend, the telephone rang. He picked it up to hear a Lancashire voice say 'Hello Rob it's your Father'. He put the phone down immediately and returned home in a state of anxiety from which he had not recovered.

Her husband's father, a Lancastrian, had died 15 years ago. Only he and her husband's immediate family ever called him Rob. She and all his friends only ever knew him as Bob. Her husband was sure that it had been his father's voice.

My feelings are that the father was concerned about his son and was trying to find any route through to him. It could be for many reasons, for example business or health. If spirit people intend to make themselves known, they will do so, and if those they wish to contact do not visit places where spirit communication is encouraged, such as a spiritualist church, they will come through a direct route; so why not a telephone call? I must add that to pick up direct communication is rare unless of course you have strong psychic awareness.

I will describe a way in which spirit communicated only recently. In March, Hazel, a very dear relative of mine passed over. We had talked together for many hours during the last days of her life and she had requested at her funeral the song *I can see clearly now*. This was particularly appropriate as her illness towards the end of her earthly life was causing her to go blind. Her son in law found the song and in due course it was played as requested at her funeral.

Two days after Hazel's death, her new granddaughter was born, and after the funeral service her daughter, son in law and Hazel's two sons went to buy the new born a present from her late grandmother. In the toy shop her daughter picked up a teddy bear and asked her husband and brothers whether they thought their mother would have liked it. Children's music was being played in the shop at the time, but it suddenly changed and they could not believe what they were hearing, for the music was *I can see clearly now*, the very music requested by their mother at her funeral. They knew that their mother was with them, and this was further reinforced when they asked about the tape being played. They were told that this particular song was not on the tape in question, it was only children's music.

Spirit moves in many ways. I know Hazel was with them and this was her way of telling them that she was there, and understood their sadness.

I know she will be looking after her granddaughter, and will guide her along her earthly pathway.

Further evidence as to how spirit can make contact in the most unexpected places follows. For my husband's 50th birthday we went with a group of people to France for a long weekend. On the Saturday evening we were having dinner, when Eric the man sitting opposite asked me about my work. As he spoke I suddenly became clairvoyantly aware of one soldier standing each side of him. I relayed what I saw to him and then wrote down some numbers which I was being given. Eric went white and told me to carry on talking. I was able to give a few more details before the image faded. Eric was amazed and went on to tell us of events that he had never told anyone before. When he had been called up for war service he had become very good friends with the men standing either side of him in the queue. They went through the war together and it was at Dunkirk that Eric saw both his friends killed on the beaches. He said that he saw the spirits rise out of their bodies and they had spoken to him telling him not to worry as they would see him safe to England,

They had walked on both sides of him, and he explained to us that he was able to walk across the beach with bullets being fired all around him; he seemed impenetrable. He had then found himself on a boat, and was brought safely back to England. It had taken him years to recover from what he had witnessed, so it was not surprising that my revelation had caused him to turn pale. After all those years his friends had come again to tell him they were around and still his mates.

When I give talks to various groups, many of the same questions arise, and one in particular is 'What do people do on the other side'? My answers come direct from the source, and I am told that spirit people can see, touch, do everything as on this plane, but they are working on a different vibrational level. They can appreciate each others company, and can attend meetings to absorb knowledge from the Elders. There are libraries and halls of learning, and what is more spirit people are free of all illness and disability with which they were burdened before death. They sense as before and are able to enjoy the flowers and gardens that surround them with ever greater beauty than anything we have ever seen. Animals also survive death and have a different vibrational level, but if a deep and loving link has been forged in this life between animal and human, then they can be together on the other side.

There are many dimensions through which the spirit can progress, and this is what the Bible terms *the second death*. When the spirit makes a further transition onto the next level it cannot then make a direct link with the earth plane, because the vibrational fields are very finely tuned. They can however send a message to the level below and this can be passed on through a guide to a sensitive on the earth plane. So, when Mediums in spiritualist churches use the term *messages*, that is just what they are. It is thought however that calling for too much spirit communication can hold back the departed soul from its natural progression, and this is why certain churches are against spirit communication.

Grief too can delay the progression of the spirit, but we who are left on the earth plane do grieve, and to have evidence of our loved one's survival is of great solace. It is good to remember however that once we have had our proof, we should send them on their way with love, not hinder their progress, knowing full well that we will be together again one day.

It is worth remembering that the social standing of people in this world does not mean anything in the next world, and I am told that this can sometimes come as quite a shock to those who have a high opinion of themselves or of their status. They feel that because of who they are, they can still demand some kind of acknowledgement, but not so, everyone is on an equal footing. I am told also that communication is direct through a mental link and so language becomes universal.

How do I get my information from the source? This is a question frequently asked of me. At one time all information was gained in seances, but now a sensitive can sit alone and tune in with the source, providing they know their guide and are certain of their protection. I work with various helpers and guides, and can sit and write the answers to the questions that I have mentally asked.

I have had the privilege of being taken onto the astral levels to see for myself, and of bringing back the information to record and pass on to those searching for answers. Some of the information I receive is very deep but perhaps in time as people develop a better understanding, I will be able to give it out. It is important that our understanding develops slowly and surely, and our growing awareness becomes a spur to seek and progress along our chosen pathway. Confusing and deeply philosophical knowledge can deter people from their quest unless they have reached a level of progression which enables them to understand it.

There will come a time for all of us to make our last contact with this earthly world, and pass through the gateway marked death. I have always compared death to a wonderful journey, a journey of enlightenment. It has always been my belief that we should know more about this journey; if we go on holiday, we book the hotel, possibly research our route and make plans for the journey. For the most incredible journey of our life most of us do not even wish to speak of it. We do not even wonder where we are going or how we are going to get there.

In Buddhist rituals you find that sermons are administered to a dying person to assist them on their final journey. The Lama will sit with the person and point him to the future. He will talk of the light and will divert all thoughts away from the material world and the family, and so help the departing soul take the special journey into the light.

The last rites which are carried out by various other Christian churches are of a similar nature to those outlined above, but they may use prayers and burn incense. The intention in all cases is to reassure the dying and help them to know that they will soon be with God. The last thought at death is of prime importance and it is always helpful whenever possible to have people in the room who are able spiritually to send loving thoughts out to the departing soul on its journey.

chapter 3
ASTRAL LEVELS AND REINCARNATION

When a person is in the astral body, whether they are recent or long departed spirits, they are operating at an increased energy level.

Sometimes the ghosts that people see are not necessarily spirits of the dead but spirits of people still in the human body but in their sleep state. For in the sleep state we can leave our bodies and go onto the astral levels.

I am asked very often how long a departed soul spends in the astral realms. This I find a little difficult to answer, for it appears that mediums and clairvoyants cannot agree. I feel that it can be as long as is desired, and it may be until loved ones on the earth plane have made their transition to the astral.

After death, everyone has to pass through several levels, and may or may not be conscious of them. I feel that because the vibration levels are different, time too is on a different scale and what would seem days to us would be only minutes to those on other levels. When people pass over to the astral level, they will see themselves as they really are; God does not judge them, they are their own judge and jury, and amends will have to be made for bad deeds committed in this life. For instance, people who have taken a life will have to redeem themselves possibly in another lifetime or even through many lifetimes. If we all were more aware of this fact, and recognised that for every criminal act we committed, however small, we would have to make amends, then maybe we would stop and think before committing any action that causes harm to others. If the law of Karma *as we sow so shall we reap* was uppermost in people's minds, then crime would become a thing of the past, and we would understand that the seeds we sow today will be reaped in future incarnations. So our lives today should be based on love and peace.

Every one of us has an appointed life span; it is a crime against nature to take one's own life. There is no death, so destroying life will not solve any problems, only add to those already acquired. The consequences of the karmic effect of suicide are severe; our lives must run their natural span whether that be a few hours or many years.

We must realise too that capital punishment is wrong. Those making the decision, or even condoning the taking of a life, are guilty of the crime of murder, for which retribution will have to be made, not always in this life, but certainly in a future lifetime. Condemning another human being to death brings with it the same responsibility as it does to those who take life in anger, hatred or revenge, for they are sending someone into the spirit world angry and afraid, and no one has this right over another person's life.

It is my firm belief that all who commit heinous crimes should in fact be deprived of their freedom in society for the rest of their natural lives on the earth plane. Their very thoughts through this time would be their punishment, and if the law of Karma was explained to them, they could start mentally working towards their next incarnation, to which they would inevitably come to redeem themselves. If all had this outlook and understanding of life, our prisons would not be full of criminals, an ever present curse on our society. However the spiritual understanding of Karma needs teaching from an early age in order that our world can become a better place.

I have had the privilege of being taken to the Astral levels, and have witnessed many things, some not always pleasant. For example, I have been shown the places where people go who have carried out terrible deeds, the level at which they must remain until they learn the error of their ways. If more people were able to experience this sight, they would think carefully before committing crimes of death and destruction.

When someone dies who has been selfish and non-caring, their style of life on the earth plane indicated that they were at a low vibrational level and had not yet progressed to the level of a sensitive human. Therefore they would go straight to an astral sub-plane where it would be the responsibility of the spirit helpers who work on that level to try and help them to progress. Should they not succeed, the spirit still working at its low vibrational level would become an entity who would relish trying to destroy others who might come under its influence on the earth plane.

Conversely, if someone has led a life of good intentions and has helped others without thought of personal reward, there will be no necessity to go through the different levels. When they pass over, such people will go straight to the astral plane to which they are attuned, the level of their own vibration, and be with their relatives and friends who will be waiting for them. It is a fact that the people we feel in harmony with on the earth plane are vibrating at the same level on the Astral levels where we will meet again. People on this level will often find that after a while they still want to work for humanity whether back in the physical body or in the spiritual realms. They could for example opt to become the spirit helpers on the lower Astral planes.

It may surprise some people to learn that we do choose our level on the earth plane before we are reborn. We choose our parents, and to some extent map out in advance, with the help of the Elders, the pathway which is ahead of us in the new physical body. The Elders are those who, vibrating on an even higher level, give guidance. When we are ready to return to the earth plane they look back with us at our past lives and see where we went wrong. If we wish to progress onwards and upwards to other realms, we must right the wrongs of our previous lives and pay off our Karmic debt. Therefore we would choose the life that would enable us to do this, which would not necessarily be an easy one. If however, in our darkest hours we could understand that we were suffering in order to progress, and that we had chosen this path specially, maybe it would make life a little easier to bear.

Orthodox Jewish, Islamic and Christian teachings have all at some point denied the existence of reincarnation, and yet looking back into the early teachings of all these religions, belief in reincarnation is evident.

There were many problems in the early Christian doctrine which caused increasing hostility towards anyone believing in reincarnation. Eventually at a point in time, the gospels were rewritten without the reincarnation aspect of the original teachings. However reading the Bible very carefully, it is possible to find references where this aspect has escaped the ruthless editing of those who wished to control the minds of followers, for example, the rebirth of Jacob and Esau is mentioned many times in both the New and Old Testaments. It is interesting to note that there is a growing awareness amongst many priests and ministers, who are now accepting that there has to be an understanding of life after death and life before birth.

People are no longer prepared to be controlled by doctrines but are beginning to question, search and want answers. I feel many religious bodies have suppressed knowledge, partly to keep people in control and prevent individual thinking, and partly because the hidden teachings of the original gospels were not fully understood. We will never know the answer for sure, but I would say to anyone, read the Bible with an open mind. Forget the instruction that has probably been instilled from an early age, although much of it was right and true, but read it again with your eyes open. See what it is saying to you as a free thinking individual; apply your own thoughts to this book of great wisdom and some of the hidden teachings may reveal themselves to you.

For those of us who accept reincarnation or who are struggling with the concept and need help or some kind of proof, what can be done to assist? Many people visit regressionists; this is usually a hypnotherapist who can take people back into previous lives often with very interesting results. Knowing who they were can help people who suffer from various illnesses, simply because weaknesses in parts of the body often reflect what has occurred in a past life. A person who had met death by drowning in a previous lifetime could have their fear of water ably explained to them, and understanding the reason often removes the fear.

Above all regression shows that people have lived many times before, and no doubt will live again. This is just one way of searching for proof, although I feel that reincarnation makes sense with or without proof. There is so much to achieve; all of us have a purpose in life, a purpose that we are not always certain of. It is going to take more than one lifetime to get it right and achieve our ultimate goal, but if we understand that this is the purpose of existence and accept the rule of Karma (the law of cause and effect) we may reach our goal a little quicker.

If we do not wish to take the opportunity to come back in the physical body, I have been told that we can stay in the spirit realms but without any chance of progression. Progression does not necessarily mean returning to the earth plane; there are other dimensions, other planets. Why should we think that we are the only people in the universe. I know that we are not, but if this is difficult to accept I can only say do not dismiss it, keep an open mind.

To summarise; becoming aware of the astral levels introduces a new outlook on life. I often think of it as being similar to a department store; there is the basement (this World), the first floor (1st Astral), second floor (2nd Astral), 3rd floor (3rd Astral) and so on. In the department store we take a lift, or an escalator through the different levels. On our journey through life we ascend through our actions, thoughts and understanding onto the higher planes of existence. I believe that eventually we will reach the highest level when we no longer need to return to continue our development.

chapter 4
SPIRIT GUIDES

I am asked numerous times why many guides seem to be Red Indians. I believe that the Red Indians were in fact remainders of a very old civilisation, and until the white man came they lived in harmony with nature and their Godhead who they called the Great White Spirit. The Indians known as the Medicine Men were equal to our clairvoyants, mediums, and healers, and this in itself could be why many guides are drawn from the orders of the Red Indians. In some cases far more highly evolved spirits use the names of Red Indians to pass their messages on to us, and in many cases will only use this name for a period of time.

There are of course many other races who communicate with the mediums working on the earth plane, and they originate from a wide range of countries such as Tibet, India, China and Egypt. In a great many instances, children play a large part in being guides, but it seems that few guides are drawn from the white race. This may be because other races and cultures seem closer to the earth and the spirit world than the white man.

I feel that it is important to stress however that we should not put these guides on a pedestal, or 'guide worship' as some clairvoyants and mediums do. I have heard certain people say 'my guide told me this and my guide says that', but to use a pun, I always feel that this could be a little misguided. I think guides would be the first to say that their work is vitally important, and that they are special helpers and messengers with tasks to fulfil together with friends on this side, but they are not to be venerated, they are not the Divine Spirit. Of course they are to be loved and respected, as you love and respect a close friend, because that is exactly what they are.

The guides with the highest ability belong to the White Brotherhood, and included amongst them is White Feather whom I have contact with from time to time and the great Silver Birch. Around them are many other highly evolved beings who devote themselves to enlightening people on the earth plane; they represent the higher Astral planes.

I have been asked in the past how and why many people can share the same guide, as it is not possible for anyone to be in different places at the same time. I assure you that our guides can, for their power is far greater than anything we mortals can imagine. Try to think of a huge diamond with many facets, the diamond being the oversoul. Imagine the facets shining out in many and various directions to radiate and enlighten the minds of men. The diamond is the whole with many facets, so the spiritual teachings are from the same oversoul but come in different forms matched to the needs of the individual receiving the communication. One guide therefore can reach many, and transmit different messages under the same name. In reality the name is unimportant, the teachings and enlightenment are all that matters; as long as the teachings are correct the name is of little concern.

These guides are real people, just more enlightened and more evolved. They are therefore further along the pathway, and I believe they give us tests to see whether we are up to standard. It depends on how we cope with their test as to whether they work with us or pass us on to another teacher or guide. Guides also have to be taught for like us they cannot demand what they do. They can offer their services for mankind and then they too are put through various tests in the spirit world. I believe that the hardest part for them is finding someone on the earth vibration to tune in to, for 'like attracts like', and one guide may be able to work with one medium whereas another would find communication impossible. I know that I have had several people working with me from time to time, and in some cases they have been my friends who have died. My own father helped me for a while, and my mother helped me make the journey to the astral levels where I saw the great halls of learning. It was indeed a great privilege to be taken there, where I also met elders and guides who belong to the White Brotherhood, so I do speak from experience.

You will find that when a higher Master comes close to inspire us on the earth plane, he knows who he can link with, and will accept those as pupils. Before be starts on the teaching process he will take special precautions to satisfy himself that they are of a type that he can attune himself to. Because this higher Master has chosen a certain person, it does not mean that other pupils on the pathway are unacceptable, it is just that some people are a more suitable match, for one reason or another. These chosen pupils are put to the test many times to see how much they can take, and when they are ready the Master takes them in hand, and the knowledge and teaching that they receive can then be imparted to others on the earth plane. The pupil can be on this pathway for many years, even a lifetime, and perhaps many previous lifetimes have been spent working towards it. The work is being done so that we can eventually welcome the new World Teacher. The doors of the Aquarian Age are being opened for this very reason.

The New Age of Aquarius has brought different names for Mediums and Clairvoyants; the popular term at the moment for bringing through messages from another plane is *Channelling*.

A Channeller is someone who either has contact with Guides on the other side, or who is taken over by their personal Guide and the Guide speaks through them.

Most people who channel tend to be what I call Trance-Mediums. With such individuals, the person who channels is taken over or 'overshadowed'; they very rarely remember what has been said. The Guide coming through can give personal information about someone who has departed this earth, or bring through teachings from one of the Masters.

I do feel that channelling should only be done under controlled circumstances. I personally feel there could be some dangers in this kind of mediumship and care must be taken that it is not the Channeller's higher self who is relaying the information whilst firmly believing it comes from a spiritual Guide.

There is no doubt that when a Master or higher Guide does make a link, the information that can be brought through is wonderful, and you then know that this is true spirit communication.

I have frequently referred to the White Brotherhood, a brotherhood compiled of the very highly evolved souls, the Great Masters. The great man the Nazarene, is one of the Brotherhood. It is he to whom the guides turn for leadership and knowledge; he attunes direct with the Source of all things. As I understand it, there are conferences held regularly in the spirit world and discussions as how best to help the people on the earth plane. I am sure they must despair at times when their help is rejected for one reason or another.

We humans should understand that we are ruled by the law of Karma (the law of cause and effect), by rhythms and cycles of nature, and that there is only one sky above us and one Great Spirit. This Great Spirit is the one source of all things and we are all brothers and sisters under the skin. Only then, when we truly know and understand these things, will peace reign on this most beautiful planet earth. It is not our planet which is a terrible place but the inner fighting which occurs on it, perpetrated by we humans in our greed for material possessions and power over others. When we understand the teachings of the Great Masters, then love will enter the aura of the earth and engulf us all with a beautiful belonging.

chapter 5
DREAMS

Dreams have been interpreted in many ways, but what we need to understand is that the astral body never sleeps, only the physical body rests to prepare itself for further activity.

Our dreams are as real as any journey, we literally go where the spirit takes us. We all dream, and I believe that in the dream state we can go on to other Astral levels, in some cases perhaps be in touch with the Akashic records (details of all peoples' lives both past, present and future). We may indeed go into the future in our dreams, whether it be by days, months or years.

As an example I will tell you about a dream I had eight weeks before my father died. In my dream I saw my father in a coffin in what looked to be a black and white suit. Two months later my father died very suddenly and when my daughter and I saw him in the chapel of rest he was wearing a garment of black and white. I had been given some indication of what the future held and as I suggested in my previous book maybe much of our destiny is mapped out.

Sometimes our dreams do not appear to make sense. This could be a conflict between the astral and physical bodies; we are getting a confusion between this world and the astral world. There was a time when men and women were aware in their waking state of the astral, and they could see each others astral bodies. Colours could be seen very vividly and the colours of the aura surrounding each individual were plainly seen; their minds were more open and aware. This I feel will occur again in time to come, maybe the new Aquarian age is the start of it, for people are becoming more aware of colours and auras and wanting to know more about energy fields.

Often when I do platform work, I become aware of the astral bodies of the people and the colours surrounding and vibrating from them. These images help me to know the person, both mentally and physically. The state of physical health always shows up in the aura, and I am sometimes able to help people as a result of this manifestation.

It may help to understand a little more about the astral body and all that is associated with it. The astral body has colours around it which as I said earlier, can be seen by the developed clairvoyant and can extend out ten inches or so beyond the physical body. It is possible with a special camera to take photographs of auras when the colours can be clearly seen.

Young children have only a white aura around them, but as they grow and develop the colours start to appear, their differing characters determining the colours which build up around them. Some people can feel the aura of whoever is standing at their side, and sometimes auras have been known to appear on photographs or even paintings over a period of time.

Like the physical body, which is a material substance protecting the finer organs, the astral body is also a vehicle protecting finer substances and surrounded by an aura. The aura too is composed of very fine matter, in which all feeling of passions and emotions are felt and expressed. The astral body possesses a life source of its own, and in the sleep state can leave the physical body and travel freely on its own and enter the astral planes. In most cases when the astral body is reunited with the physical body on awakening, the dreamer will not remember anything about the astral journeys. When the body does remember, we think of the events as dreams.

When we return from the dream world we may occasionally come back into the physical body quite quickly, and waken up with a jolt. I am sure most people have experienced this, and many times felt they have not slept at all. This feeling can occur when there has not been time to adjust from the astral world of our dreams to the waking state of this world.

Dreams are in a way a window onto the astral world; you can sometimes find that answers to problems come through the dream state. I firmly believe that there are parts of our lives which we are meant to know about if we take the trouble to investigate and learn, but there are other matters we are not given access to. If we are meant to know the answer and we are genuine and sincere in our search, then the answer will come, but not always in the way we expect.

I have already mentioned the Akashic Records; these records concern every living thing, not only here but also in other worlds. They are a form of vibration, a little like television or radio energy waves, full of knowledge of what has been and what will be. A Medium or Clairvoyant, or indeed anyone who is psychic, can attune their state of consciousness to tap into the records or energy waves. A psychic who is telling a person about their past life is tapping into the Akashic records to gain the information. As I indicated, I believe that anyone who has the patience and is prepared to practise, can tune in, although it can happen quite naturally in the dream state. It is very important that as these psychic abilities develop and a way is found to lift the higher self to link with these energy waves, that we do not let the ego take over. Such abilities are privileges not party tricks.

Not all dreams are the result of astral journeys, some are our own deeply subconscious thoughts surfacing in the relaxed state of sleep. Sometimes a particularly harrowing experience either of real life or witnessed on film or television can have a deep effect on the subconscious, and can surface again as a nightmare for the sleeper. Children in particular find these dreams a regular occurrence, and wherever possible should be protected from witnessing anything too traumatic for their young minds to understand. Horror films especially can have long term effects on the young subconscious mind.

I am often asked how we can tell whether a dream is a result of an astral journey, or a trip into our subconscious, and this is not easy to answer. Astral dreams are usually forgotten more quickly, but when remembered there is a distinct feeling that this was no ordinary dream. Often a dream memory can be sparked by an incident just occurring, and the mental reaction is 'that has broken my dream', or 'that has happened before'. Often *déja vous* experiences can be a result of earlier astral journeys in the dream state. The jumbled dream, often remembered plainly on waking, and linking vaguely with ongoing incidents in life, has usually been a trip into the subconscious. Even going to bed on a particularly full stomach can trigger bad or disturbed dreams.

However there are no hard and fast ways of knowing which dreams are meaningful; all we need is an awareness that our dreams can be significant, and that we must keep an open mind. This way, what needs to be made known to us will surely be understood. I would advise anyone to keep a pen and paper at the bedside, and to record their dreams, for at some future time, maybe even in years to come, the events could make a lot of sense.

chapter 6
MEDITATION

With the increased interest in alternative medicine and the medical profession looking more widely into, for example, the power of the mind through the use of hypnotherapy, the beneficial effects of stilling the mind as in meditation are becoming apparent.

It can be difficult to decide which meditation method is best for each individual, but I do believe that when it comes to searching for a way, each person is led to what suits them best. Eastern Yoga is perhaps the best known and is concerned with bringing the body into harmony and lifting the consciousness through bodily movement and position.

Some of the physical techniques employed are:

Posture: How one is seated is important as are the positions of the hands, feet and body.

Deep relaxation: This exercise is a conscious one in order to relax the muscles with deep rhythmic breathing. It helps to focus the attention on the higher self.

Mantras: Chanting certain phrases helps to focus the attention on to vibrations, which in turn helps to bring the mind and body into harmony.

Spiritual meditation concentrates on lifting the level of the mind without the use of physical activity. There are many pathways, two examples of which are:

1. A group of like minded people sit together. Visualisation and the use of symbols creates a harmonising effect amongst the people who are sitting together. In doing this they can seal the *Aura* around the group, which has the effect of keeping out any lower spirits who may try to come into the circle.

2. Again a circle of people may be assembled, and a leader of the group can talk people through a symbolic journey, using peaceful scenes often of great beauty, bringing the visualisation techniques into play again. The purpose of this mental imagery is to invoke the higher self. There can, I feel be some dangers in this, and unless the leader is very experienced I would not personally recommend it.

Unless the leader is in control the more sensitive people in the circle may experience events which may not always be good for them, and may even be sent on journeys from which it is not always easy to return. An experienced leader is always in control and watchful of those under their guidance. They know the limits beyond which it would be foolish to go with such a group of people.

The whole purpose of meditation and yoga is to make the mind a friend, and to aim for self-realisation, to link to the higher levels and to the Godhead. The aim should be to spend a few minutes each day attuning the spiritual senses with the absolute. To do this a special place should be found and always returned to for meditation.

It does not matter what religion you are, whether Christian, Hindu, Jew or Muslim, anyone can meditate and it will help with everyday life. It will assist with harmonising the energies and help cope with problems of the material world.

Every religion does in fact meditate in its own way, be it through prayer, chanting or silent devotion. Does it matter in the end how it is carried out as long as it brings peace within, and does not harm others?

Yoga will give self esteem, it helps balance natural energies, but you will need to contribute determination, faith and above all love. Many people use Yoga and meditation as a journey of self discovery; it gives a new way of looking at life. It is a journey that is normally taken alone, and leads to higher levels of awareness and inner satisfaction. It can reveal the higher spiritual side of a person and when a certain stage of development has been reached the individual's spiritual guide will appear to give help and guidance along the pathway.

As we are all individuals, so through meditation we can become one with the Godhead, or whatever name you choose to use for the Source of all things. It is a lone journey, for it is the soul's journey and will lead from the material world back to the spiritual world. Through meditation we come to understand that the world in which we live our daily lives is in reality only a shadow of the real thing.

chapter 7
THE HIDDEN DANGERS

When we tread the pathway of psychic and spiritual unfoldment, we should be aware that dangers do exist. I will outline some aspects of these dangers from my point of view by relating some of my own experiences in this field, and how these have made me aware of the vital need for spiritual protection.

Over the years many books have been written about spiritual possession; some people do not want to accept that possession is possible while others prefer to turn a blind eye to it.

Let me give an instance. When someone of bad character dies, as I have explained in the Astral Levels chapter, he will not become perfect immediately the transition occurs. Even worse, if he does not accept he has died, he will try to attach himself to someone on the earth plane who is of like mind. Anyone of dubious character, dabbling with something like the ouija board for example, would become a prime target for possession by this low spirit.

Whatever method is used, whether as a Medium, Tarot reader, Clairvoyant or in any other areas of the psychic field, channels are being opened up. Unless the right guides and helpers are working on the other side, these channels are open for unwanted entities to come close. These entities of bad intent can drain energy from the person working, and this can happen even to those who are unaware of their psychic abilities and are opening channels without realising it. Children are particularly vulnerable, as most children have psychic ability, and at times when they are possibly in some way mentally or emotionally disturbed, their channels may be opened to undesirable entities.

I feel that too many people are dismissive of these possibilities. As so many are now searching for truth and investigating the psychic pathways, perhaps sitting in circle or similar, without any understanding of the need for protection, they could be attracting entities of undesirable intent. Having once attracted them, they then have no idea how to get rid of them.

There is the old saying *like attracts like*, and that goes for the spirit world as well as the earth plane. This is a disturbing area of psychic awareness but one which should not to be dismissed. It is also one reason for the church being against contact with spirit, and working in this field, I must admit I can understand some of the reasoning.

In recent months I have been asked to go to houses which have in the words of the occupants been *haunted*. Even with my knowledge and experience, if I am particularly tired or unwell, I can let my energy be misused and sometimes attract unwanted entities around me. I am fortunate that at such times when I know myself to be vulnerable, I have a colleague who is psychically very strong, and I can pass people with problems over to him. I am so grateful for this, for I could not deal with all the calls I get, and it is important that we realise our own vulnerability, have some humility and understand that our power is not infallible. We must never allow a sense of our own importance to get in the way, or the gift we have will be misused and do harm to others as well as to ourselves. Sometimes I have made people smile because I use the expression 'I cannot help, but I know a man who can'. A sense of humour is another important requisite for this type of work!

I will give some examples of my working experiences and it should then become clear how unwanted entities can interfere with our lives, and sometimes cause great difficulties.

A lady got in touch with me on behalf of her mother in law, and I went alone to her house. Going on my own was a mistake, the lady had been experiencing spirit activity around her for quite some time. Whatever was there was quite threatening and in one instance had pulled a blanket off a bed, and in another had actually pulled someone out of the bed. These spirit beings had in fact followed her around from one house to another, and in each house there had been problems.

I sat and talked with her for a while and discovered that in the past, she had asked a vicar to come and exorcise her home. This seemed to cause even more problems, and it is not the first time I have known this to have happened. We chatted further and I discussed with her what I felt she should do, but when I left the house and got home I felt exhausted. This is quite normal for me after having faced problems like this, but this time it was much worse than usual.

Eventually I rang my colleague and he came to see me. I too needed re-energising after the experience and I felt better after his visit. I realised however that this was one situation that I should not handle and asked my friend to take it over for me. This he did, and in fact saw the lady two or three times, and I am pleased to say she has had no problems since.

It is important that we do not see our own inability to handle certain cases as failures. The failure would have been in not recognising the signs and going ahead, possibly with very negative results. Our purpose is to help, not to go on personal ego trips.

I was asked to go to a flat in Church Hill, Redditch, but this time I decided not to go on my own. I asked my friend to meet me there and we met the young lady occupier, who had a son aged about two years old. She was experiencing and seeing a small spirit boy, who had also been seen by at least two others. The lady had seen him looking over her own little boy, had experienced pictures falling off walls for no apparent reason and had heard knocks on the wall. The child she saw was aged about four, and the whole affair was proving very frightening for her. We were able to put her mind at rest, and made contact with the spirit boy. Often it is just a case of gently helping a spirit to progress and move onwards in the astral realms. Sometimes it is necessary to ask your own spirit guides and helpers to assist with this task. Fortunately after our visit the lady had no further problems.

A quite exceptional case occurred some years ago, when I again made the mistake of going alone. One day I had a frantic telephone call from a lady in the Woodrow area of Redditch; she asked if I could visit her and two of her friends as they believed they had a ghost around them.

One lady's house had been the first focal point; children's clothes had been seen to fly up in the air and rooms had felt extremely cold. At first it was taken lightly, but then another lady had problems in her house, such as the lights flashing, clothes going missing and turning up in someone else's airing cupboard.

Then at yet another house problems started to occur. It was so bad that I was getting phone calls at midnight, 6.00 in the morning, and then at all times of day and night. Once again I turned to my friend for help. I have no doubt that in difficult cases, the stronger the psychic presence the more help is needed, and there is certainly safety in numbers.

Occasionally either one of us would go alone but usually we went together. On one occasion I witnessed shadows walking around the room, and by now these girls and their children were all sleeping in one house in one room, they had become so scared. Then one morning I had a call from my colleague. He said that he had been over to visit the houses and felt that he had brought 'something' home with him; now it was my turn to return the favours and go to help him. Between us we did eventually sort the problems out and up to now there have been no more phone calls from these girls.

The fact that you are reading this book, means that you are embarking on a search to understand the unknown. These instances of unnerving psychic occurrences, which even I and others like me were affected by, should serve to emphasise the importance of not dabbling with the unknown. It may prove difficult to handle and end with very unpleasant results.

chapter 8
FURTHER GHOST HUNTING

There have been so many houses and people I have visited over the last few years, that it is difficult to recall them all, but here are some more examples.

The Woodrow area of Redditch seems to have more than its fair share of paranormal activity. I have become friends with a lady who phoned me from this area asking for help, as she never felt happy in the home that she was occupying. It had started with her dog not wanting to go into the house; it used to bark and howl, and she generally had problems with him. I believe that eventually they were obliged to find another home for him.

Then her little girl, aged about 2 years old, became unsettled and began to talk in a different language in her sleep. The child's grandparents came to visit and her grandfather, although alone in the house at the time, thought he could hear someone talking in the hall. Thinking that the others had returned home early he went to investigate, but there was no one there. The whole family heard voices at one time or another, and they were always having problems with the electrics. One area of the house was always freezing cold.

Misfortune dogged the family and eventually they decided that they would have to move from the house. Before leaving, the lady spoke to a neighbour about her reasons for moving, and it appeared that no-one had lived in that particular house for very long, and that other houses in that row had experienced strange phenomena. Living where they do now they are much happier and everything seems to be going well for them. They have had no further psychic happenings, and my feeling is that the problem is not with the people, but with the area on which that particular estate is built.

Far too much occurs in this locality which is beyond normal explanation. It has been said that a man in gaiters walks through the centre at night, and has been seen by many people. It is interesting to note that the local High School is called the Leys High School. Any connection I wonder with Ley Lines? (page 50)

I was told about a young girl who moved onto the same estate, and who had terrible problems when she was in her house. The lights would continually go on and off and she saw a shadow on the staircase. Eventually she persuaded a friend to stay the night and he too witnessed the events. On speaking to a neighbour about the occurrences, they were asked if they had ever looked in the loft. There had been no reason to do so, but they now made it their business to investigate. When the loft was opened they found black magic symbols and candles. The young lady left the house immediately, and I believe never returned. I never did find out what happened to the house, or whether subsequent occupants experienced anything strange.

Another case brought to my attention was of a family on the Farm Road side of Redditch. They had been having problems with electrical equipment such as the television and washing machine. They had heard knockings and had felt a 'presence' around them and had consequently called in a Vicar. He suggested they burn the wardrobe because he felt the problems were linked to it, but in my opinion the suggestion would not help the situation.

The wardrobe had belonged to the lady's grandmother who had recently died. I was sure that if it was the grandmother causing the problems she certainly would not mean any harm to a family whom she loved. I told them not to burn the piece of furniture, and advised them to wait while I sought help for their grandmother. I asked my guides and helpers to assist the old lady with her transition onto the astral planes, and I am glad to say there have been no further problems.

There was a house down Marsden Road, which I was once asked to visit, again I was following in the footsteps of the Vicar. The family had heard footsteps going up and down the stairs, and had heard a sound like the banging of a walking stick. The front bedroom always felt extremely cold no matter how it was heated. They had even asked the council for a transfer to another house because they were so frightened. On arrival at the house I went upstairs and sat in the front bedroom, and almost immediately felt the presence of an old man. I mentally spoke to him, telling him to let himself go from the earth plane, because there was a better life for him, and he must move on and progress. I put some flowers and a small cross in the room. A few weeks later I met the couple in town, and they told me that there had been no further problems; in consequence they decided against moving house. In fact the house was now very peaceful and they were extremely happy to be there. Not all cases are as easy to handle as that, I only wish they were.

On another occasion I was asked to visit a young lady who had recently inherited a house from her father. She had been experiencing many strange happenings such as the television changing channels, footsteps on the stairs and in the bedroom, doors opening and closing, and again, one room was always icy cold. Feeling that there could be a strong spirit presence I played safe and asked my friend to go with me. Both of us felt that it was the lady's father who was still around, and I was tuning in to him quite strongly. I discovered by conversing mentally with him, that he was trying to warn his daughter not to sell the house. We then discovered that she had in fact been approached only that week by a builder wanting her to sell. When she realised that it was her father trying to help her, she was no longer afraid and seemed rather glad that he was still involved with her life. Others I suppose could resent such activity as interference, but in this case the father-daughter relationship was obviously very strong. After we left the various happenings ceased, and I might add, the house was not sold.

Some years ago I went to visit an interesting house in Alcester. On arrival the owner asked me to walk around this extremely old building dating back to the early seventeenth century, and although it was now two houses, it used to be only one. It was said that Queen Victoria stayed there when she was the Princess of Kent. I walked around this lovely house with its small passage ways and twisted stairs, and then entered one bedroom. I immediately felt very strange and became very cold. I had a tingling feeling up and down my spine, and the lady of the house told me that many people were similarly affected on entering this particular room.

What had happened in this room was quite remarkable and in a way a little frightening. The lady's son had slept in the bedroom when they had first moved into the house, and had kept waking up with a nightmare. He said that he could see a young girl dressed in old clothes with her arms outstretched as if wanting him to help her, her face was burnt and black and there was a terrible stench in the room. Bearing in mind that no-one else could see this vision, the family assumed it was indeed just a nightmare. After several nights of this recurring dream, the boy's mother realised that there was possibly more to it than just a bad dream, so she set about doing some research. On delving into the history of the house she discovered that there had been a serious fire and a young servant girl had burnt to death in the area of the house which was now this bedroom.

Understandably they moved the boy to another bedroom and his nightmares ceased. The interesting sequel was that the lady's husband occasionally slept in the same bedroom and was never affected, in fact he always seemed to have a good night's sleep! This goes to show that some people are more sensitive than others, children in particular. My feeling is that this young boy was not actually seeing a ghost but was tapping into a time warp, rather like an action replay of what had occurred all those years previously, and only he was able to experience it.

I went to another cottage where the owners were experiencing the usual happenings. The husband had walked in to the kitchen and seen an old lady dressed in Victorian clothes, who then just seemed to vanish. Doors opened and closed when there was no one about and footsteps had been heard walking across the bedroom. There was of course the inevitable ice cold room. The cottage was in fact two smaller ones made into one, and the owners had always felt uneasy living there. On investigation they discovered that some years previously, a lady had hanged herself in one of the cottages. The Victorian ghost seen by the husband could well have been this lady, still holding on to the earth plane. Suicides can often be the cause of disturbing psychic activity, probably because of the traumatic state of mind on passing, and perhaps due to the fact that they have taken their own lives before their appointed time.

Some years ago I had a young man get in touch with me, who asked me to go to his girl friend's house in Shirley, Warwickshire. He told me that they were experiencing a lot of things happening both to them and the house. It emerged through conversation that he had bought a black Ford Escort car from a scrap-yard, and he was doing it up in the garage attached to the house. He told me that he was not a bit psychic, but whenever he was working on the car he always felt as though he had someone standing at his back, watching him.

I arranged to meet them and took another friend, Elsie, along with me. We felt from the time we first arrived at the house that it had a negative feel to it and that it was a house where nothing seemed to go right. We went into the garage where there were bits of the car all over the place, and the young man told us that every time he tried to fit a part, even though it was the correct one, it would never go on. He had been at the end of his tether, he told us, and was getting quite nervous about the whole thing, until his next door neighbour who was very handy with cars offered to work on it while they went on holiday.

Thankfully they went away for a few days, believing all would be sorted out on their return. However they were met by a very alarmed neighbour, who told them that a most unnerving thing had happened to him. He too had felt that someone was standing at his side, and had disliked the feeling so much that he left the garage to go back to his own house. On his own drive he had a car which was kept under covers and had not been driven for a long time. It was locked up and had no key in the ignition, yet as he passed this car, and went to enter his garage, the car suddenly started up and pinned him against the garage door. This petrified him and he was convinced that this incident was connected with the car he had been working on next door; he never worked on the Escort again.

Whilst in the garage I became aware of the strong presence of a youth, and felt certain he had met his death in an accident. I suggested that the young man who owned the Escort, should find out more about its history. By making enquiries at the scrap-yard he discovered that the car had been involved in an accident, where two young men had died. He was told that the driver had been given the car as a birthday present, and had been killed two weeks later. We all felt that this young driver was still around and was making it perfectly clear that he did not want the car on the road.

Eventually the car was sold, and the couple have heard since that it has changed hands two or three times. I still see this young couple and we talk very often about the experiences they had with the car.

Some years ago I was visiting a friend's flat when she said her neighbour, who lived upstairs, would like to speak to me as they had a ghost in the house. Linda brought her neighbour, who to my surprise was an old school friend of mine. She has three daughters, the youngest of which had seen an old lady in the kitchen. The family had also experienced taps turning themselves on and off, the toilet flushing, and even more frightening events occurring. A night-dress, which had been left on the settee over night, was found in the morning spread out on the floor with the middle part burnt out of it.

On another occasion, a friend saw a mirror, which they had just bought, lift up off the table, hit the wall and amazingly not break. There were numerous other instances relayed to me, and I began to feel that the problems were caused by the area on which the flats were built. I knew that some old property had been demolished to make way for the new flats, and perhaps someone who had lived before on that site was still around. The old lady may not have approved of what was going on in her former home, and perhaps she was trying to drive the residents away.

The following story was told to me by a neighbour of mine Mrs. Margaret Smith, who before coming to live in the village lived in Birmingham; the following are her words.

'When I was a young teenager 40 years ago, my family, mother, father and four brothers, lived in a house which I will say was haunted. We had only lived in the house for a few months when 'things' started to happen. I was sleeping up in the attic, and one night I heard someone coming up the stairs and thought it was my Mother. I called out two or three times to see who it

was, but got no reply. I jumped out of bed and put the light on but nobody was there. This happened quite a lot, and one night I felt the floor boards vibrate as though someone very heavy was walking across the floor, and my bed started to shake as the vibrations went across the floor boards. I just screamed with fright and ran down stairs to my Mother and Father, I was terrified.

After that I got my mattress off my bed and slept in my parents room for 6 months until it was decided that I should sleep in the back bedroom and my brothers would go in the attic. One night I was in bed reading a book about 10.00 pm and I heard a scratching in the fireplace. We had old fireplaces in the bedrooms at that time and I looked to see if it was a mouse. I could not see anything, so I got back into bed and then I heard the floor board creak outside the bedroom door. I called out 'Who is it?', and a man's voice called my name three times. It sounded like it was being shouted down a hollow log but the voice was definitely a man's. I looked at the door and the handle turned first one way then the other way. I was very frightened but I jumped out of bed and ran to the door pulling it open; there was no-one outside. My mother and father were down stairs watching television, and my brothers were in bed asleep. I was the only one to have heard the voice.

I would also be in the house on my own sometimes and would hear lots of voices, very loud at times. It was as though I was surrounded by a large crowd. We had a dog who would not go down into the cellar, his hair would stand on end and he would bare his teeth and growl. My mother and father said they saw a shadow of a man in a top hat and cloak on the bedroom wall. (They did not tell me until some time after it happened because of me being so afraid).

My eldest brother had a motor bike at this time and my uncle Howard always wanted my brother to take him for a ride on this motor bike. My Uncle was not well at the time so my brother said he would take him when he was better. One night when we were in bed my mother said she and my father heard the horn on my brother's motor bike go three times. They got out of bed to see who was in the shed where my brother kept his bike, all they could see was a grey mist around the shed which my mother had thought most strange, nor was there any sign of anyone around. Next day my Auntie Kate came to tell us that my Uncle had died the night before, and as he was being taken into hospital in the ambulance he kept saying he wanted to see my Mother. The next door neighbours at that time said they too had heard the horn and got out of bed, and they also had seen the mist around the shed.

My eldest brother had the attic as his bedroom and said before he went into the Army that he had felt the bed clothes being pulled off him and also had seen a light in one corner of the bedroom, but did not tell anyone because he did not want us frightening any more. The neighbours told my parents of 'things' going on in their houses as well such as noises, door handles being turned and knocking on doors. Mrs Tovey one of the neighbours said she had heard a noise on her landing as though someone was jumping up and down but could not see anyone.

I was making the beds one very hot day and was in the front bedroom. Suddenly I felt a cold gust, and I felt a very chilly feeling go straight through my body. I looked at the window thinking it was a breeze blowing through, but the net curtain was quite still.

My friend Jean who lived up the road said she too had seen a shadow on her wall of a man in a top hat and cloak. We also used to hear the front door open and close as if someone had entered through the door, but no-one was there and the door was always locked in any case.

My father was ill all the time we lived in that house, and my mother disliked the house especially as I was so afraid all the time I lived there. Once when my father was ill my mother called the doctor and he told my mother to move house. He said we would not come to any good there, and asked my mother if she knew that the houses had been built on a old cemetery. We were not aware of this at all. He said to my mother that I was a highly strung child and anaemic.

However to this day I will say that what I have written down is true, and it all happened as I said. When my mother and father moved away to another house they found out that a brother and two sisters had died in their previous house, and when we moved, the dog who was so afraid of the old cellar, would run up and down the cellar of the new house all day, without any fear at all.'

This was the end of my neighbour's story, and I would like to say that I have come across a great many similar stories which are no doubt true. I do feel that the happenings in most cases are related to the ground on which the houses are built.

Some years ago a close friend of mine Anne Girling, who had previously been my employer, started a business up in Ghana. Anne had spent some time back in England, and we very often went out together for lunch. The day before she was due to go back to Ghana I left her with a deep feeling of sadness, not just the feeling one gets on saying good-bye to a friend. On returning home I decided to write her a letter so that she would receive it immediately she arrived back in Ghana.

A symbol had appeared to me clairvoyantly, so I drew it on a piece of paper. I 'saw' colours which I put down in order and in the letter I told Anne that although they meant nothing to me, I felt that this symbol and colours would mean something to her. What followed then was quite amazing. Anne at first did not understand the symbol but she showed the letter to her gardener, who took it to one of his Elders. The Elder understood immediately. He told the gardener that a lady of great power in another country had drawn it, and it was a symbol used in Ghana to warn of bad business deals, and bad partnerships. It emerged that my friend was indeed being deceived in her business affairs and the symbol had drawn her attention to it so that the problem could be tackled.

In another incident while Anne was in Ghana, she had given me a photograph and asked me if I would do some psychometry on it. The photograph was of three people, Anne's secretary, the British High Commissioner and a Ghanaian businessman. As soon as I held the photograph I 'saw' a spirit visitor wearing full tribal dress and carrying a spear decorated with feathers. He gave me some messages to pass on to the businessman in the photograph. Anne explained that the spirit making contact was the businessman's father, who had been a tribal chief and had passed over the previous month. Anne herself had attended the burial and the chief had been buried in full tribal dress. The spear that I had seen had been given to the son, the businessman, after the burial.

My links with Anne are quite remarkable; if I focus and concentrate on her, a letter arrives and vicè versa. When she has problems I seem to sense her feelings and write to her just when she needs some help.

I have more to tell. This experience was recorded by Mrs Sonja F Mills, who I met at a house some time ago when I was talking about various supernatural subjects. She has kindly typed the following out for me .

We came to Redditch in July 1981, so during the ensuing summer months we liked to explore the local countryside. This particular summer (1987) with our son Alan now in the RAF, John (my husband) and Sarah (my daughter) we set off one Sunday afternoon for a drive,

We found ourselves at Tardebigge and as we like many other people, are fascinated by old churches, we stopped at this church and wandered in beautiful warm sunshine through the rambling, in places overgrown, but picturesque gardens and graveyard.

A quite mysterious air hung over everything. John and Sarah seemed unaware of this and chattered on exclaiming at each discovery. My mood deepened into a sort of 'mild fear' as I looked up at the high stone church which dominated the surrounding countryside and commanded beautiful views. I felt suddenly cold. The sky which was in fact clear blue, seemed to darken and I thought I could see rocks and stones hurtling down from the tower or steeple of the church. Those stone balls were breaking off and crashing down and the roof of the church was caving in.

Sarah's voice came through to me 'Mother what on earth is the matter'.

I tried to tell them what I had imagined, John quietly persuaded me to leave the churchyard. We drove down to the canal and walked along its bank. All the time I was aware of the church, it seemed to have a powerful aura and was trying to draw me back. One part of me wanted to go back, but I fought against this feeling. Eventually we went home to tea and I tried to forget the incident as being silliness on my part.

However it was to have a sequel. Some weeks later, I can't remember how many, maybe early Autumn, John bought a book from a library sale, WORCESTERSHIRE by L.T.C.ROLT first published in January 1949.

As John read the book he came across an article about Tardebigge Church which made him exclaim out loud. He showed me the article and I quote:

"On 3rd September 1775 the tower of the ancient church fell, crashing through the roof and damaging the whole structure beyond repair, so that the church which now looks down upon New Wharf from its commanding height belongs to the late eighteenth century. Just inside the main gates the Queen of the Gypsies is buried".

This in itself might not seem so remarkable, the coincidence if you choose to call it that, is September 3rd happens to be my birth date.

I was later told that the Queen of the Gypsies was killed by that fall but I cannot substantiate this and therefore doubt its truth.

My view of this is that Mrs Mills had a previous life around 1775, maybe she lived in this area and perhaps she was the Queen of the Gypsies. Maybe she had an experience of inherited memory, but we can never be sure as these things can never be proven. All we know is that she experienced an event which had been frozen in time. Why only she saw the 'video replay' we can only surmise.

I would like to relate something which happened to a family I met through my work as a clairvoyant some years ago. They live in the Winyates area of Redditch and on more than one occasion had seen a lady wearing a flimsy white dress with what appeared to be a shawl wrapped round her. Her appearances only lasted a second or two but the ghost seemed to play with the family by moving articles of clothing around, and on one occasion milk was found to be tipped on its side in the fridge when there was no logical reason for it to have occurred. On another occasion a piece of paper flew up in the air and seemed to float around the room. The paper was picked up and put into a book, but when the family returned to the room it was on the floor again. There are flats built nearby and I understand that a young girl who lived there had committed suicide; before her untimely death she had been a regular visitor to the house in question.

Was it the ghost of this girl causing all the activity, or were the family tapping into some kind of energy field? These are questions which can never be answered with certainty.

Although much of my work is carried out in the Redditch area, my telephone is always ringing from people needing help, not only in the Redditch area, but from all over the country.

One call was from a man who traced my name through the Psychic News. He lived with his father in an old farm house, and he was aged about 45 years. He had never married and had always helped on the farm, but when his mother died he had begun to experience knocking on the wall of his bedroom, always about the same time of 3.00 am. The farm house was an old building, but never before had he experienced anything strange in the house. He talked on the phone for about an hour but I was so far away I just could not help him. However I gave him the telephone number of his local spiritualist church and suggested that he went there for help.

About two weeks later I received another call from him thanking me for my help. He told me that he had found a Medium who was helping him. She had made contact with his mother, and had been able to pass on a message from her. Since then the farm had resumed its usual peacefulness.

Recently I received a telephone call from a lady in Birmingham; she had seen a spirit in her house, and was quite frightened. As I was without a car at the time, she was again too far away for me to visit. I felt very sorry for her. She was so desperate that she offered to pay for a taxi to come and collect me. I suggested the local spiritualist church might help, but she did not want to be involved, so I suggested that she contact the local vicar. I am delighted to say that he was able to help her, and the lady rang to report that all was now well. Although I have commented in previous extracts on the inability of some vicars to help solve the problems, this is not always the case, and we must be aware of all avenues that are open to us in this work.

Some years ago a lady came to see me for a reading. She was going through a messy divorce and I told her that I could see her marrying again quite quickly. I also had the name Veronica together with various other names and dates. I told her that a bracelet would be bought for her which in itself would be most unusual, and I also described a house I could see her living in. At the time none of this made sense.

About two years later the lady came again, and began to tell me of the outcome. The divorce went through, she met someone else and was married quite quickly. They moved into a house just as I had described, and one evening when her new husband came home from work he had brought her a present of an antique bracelet. She was so fascinated by what I had said about the gift of jewellery that she went to the antique shop where the bracelet had been purchased. She was told that the bracelet had been bought when a house and contents were sold, and on asking the whereabouts of the house it turned out to be the very house she was living in.

Does it surprise you to learn that the previous owner of the house to whom the bracelet had belonged, was called Veronica. This lady, who insisted she was not at all psychic, has since felt the presence of a lady around her. She has smelled lavender and feels she is being looked after and protected. It appears that the bracelet had come home.

Some people say you cannot tap into the future, but it appears I can from time to time.

I do feel that the veil between this world and the next is getting thinner, and that more people are becoming aware of this fact, and becoming conscious of spirit activity. I believe that in most cases the people from the next world are just trying to help and guide us along our way, and sometimes perhaps they are upset when we ignore them or become frightened of their communication with us on this side of the veil. If in fact this is true and the veil is getting thinner, then we should try to think of such experiences as 'normal', not 'paranormal', and maybe some of our fears will subside.

Ghost sightings are becoming more of an every day event; many people do not want to get rid of their ghosts but only to understand more about them. I find it quite comforting to have 'someone' around me, and accept them as they accept me. I am often asked how I can tell if there is a ghost present, and it is usually by a feeling of coldness, a definite change in temperature.

It was interesting to note that in the shopping centre which I mentioned in my last book, the guards often noticed a change in temperature, and saw sudden temperature drops on their monitors which could not be explained.

For those who have not read my book *Ann Jones A Way of Life*, a lot of psychic activity is evident in this particular shopping precinct, possibly because it was built over a graveyard, and there was much demolition of churches and old buildings prior to its construction.

To conclude, some of us are more sensitive than others to the different vibrations of the astral. Some of us therefore are more able to 'see' or experience psychic activity. On occasions however, not always explicably, energy fields can for a brief moment in time vibrate to a different level, which enables someone in the human body to tune in to the same level and witness whatever activity is happening. I believe that the human potential for such communication is increasing, and those on the other side whose job it is to help and guide humanity will no longer always need to do their work through mediums and clairvoyants.

chapter 9
PLANET EARTH

When we realise that the planet earth is a living being with a nervous system, that it feels and thinks, only then will we start to respect this beautiful world in which we live and have our being. Like ourselves, the earth responds to hurt and damage, so when man blows it up, rips great parts from it, buries terrible toxic waste in it, it feels the hurt and reacts. It responds as our bodies would, but planet earth's responses are through earthquakes, volcanic eruptions, tidal waves and holes in the ozone layer to mention only a few. We must also realise that the planet not only supports life, but the spiritual dimensions are all interwoven within nature, and nature reacts to the discord that we are now experiencing on the earth plane.

Regardless of what most people think we are constantly evolving towards a perfection which will entail our consciousness linking with God consciousness, but this will only come about when religions realise there is only one 'God'. There are many paths to the Godhead and all are aiming for the same perfection; the animosity and hatred between differing religions is wrong. Perhaps we should all prepare for a one world religion when all can live in peace.

With the new Aquarian age now with us, people are turning to some other kind of belief, and searching for answers not provided by the orthodox religions. This searching is leading to the awakening of the earth's energies discussed later in *Ley Lines*, which in turn is awakening the minds of men to an inner enlightenment. I feel the New Age is unfolding very quickly, so it is vital to follow the inner feeling and search for the light. If everyone pulled together and channelled the positive energies of the planet, the earth would be a better place for our children and grandchildren to live on.

We should always be aware of the power of prayer. It is tremendous and lifts the spirit; just imagine if every single one of us used this enormous power for the good of mankind and the planet on which we live, what peace and love would come through from the source of the Universe. Never forget that God is energy, God is love; both energy and love are indestructible. Love is a vital component of life so make it the mainstay of everyday living. Love is easy to give to those close to us, but we must learn to give love to all, unreservedly and unselfishly; it will be returned to us a thousand fold.

PAGANISM

What is Paganism? I feel that the roots of paganism have never really left us. Over the past hundred or so years it seems to have been ignored, but has it? Many of these ancient beliefs have actually been masked by the Christian Church. Many of the beliefs were forced underground by the fear of persecution. But in today's enlightened (we hope) world, people are wanting to know about their roots, to understand more, and along with information about the Druids, the knowledge is beginning to come to light.

The Pagan way has always been close to nature, close to humanity, the pagan way is not fixed nor dictatorial; it comes alive with music and beauty. This way recognises all things, it recognises that we are ruled by the laws of cause and effect. Pagans believe that we have had many lives and lived in many bodies to learn the *Ancient Wisdom*. A Pagan has a love for all living things, and knows that some animals are wiser than the human. A Pagan has always recognised that there is a Divine Force (God), and for many thousands of years this force has been given many names. Paganism teaches that this Highest source is both male and female,

The Pagans are of the old Religion; they know their Goddess the Mother Earth, and they know their God. They have no need for one of the new religions, for to them, they have the truth and they listen for this truth in the wind, in the rain, in the earth. They are sons and daughters of the Mother Earth.

Where do they gather? They gather in the earth's natural cathedrals, when the stars shine, deep in the forest, under the Moon, in the rocks and on the mountains. They have been driven out of the public places but the Pagan way is a society where people are free to worship. They do not believe that there are different Gods for different people, but just as there is only one sky above all of us also there is only one God. The Pagan is one who knows the pathway, one who knows the power of ritual and prayer and knows how to attune himself to the Higher self. He realises that God, if approached through the right channels, at the right time and in the right place is accessible directly by prayer. There is nothing unusual about this as the Christian Churches use the same type of rituals in their churches and meeting places; they have absorbed the pagan practices. The Pagan realises that this world is governed by various 'tides' or energy forces, and learns to bring them together; he knows this harmonises with the laws of nature. The Pagan learns to abide by the rule of love, and knows that he must return to the old way of living for people to come together once more and not be divided.

Throughout time, the four seasons have symbolised man and woman's journey through life. The spring symbolises rebirth, summer the growing of the harvest, autumn the release of the ripe fruit. The Winter, the longest night, is a time for preparation, planning, seeds to be gathered for the sowing of the new year. Most religions celebrate these festivals one way or another, the old ways masked by the new ones.

Prayer is important to the Pagan, and if all religions prayed together to one God and not separately to their own personal God, imagine the power and the love which would penetrate the planet for all to share. Man destroys man, but man cannot destroy the truth, and one way or another the truth is kept alive. *The Divine Wisdom* cannot be destroyed.

LEY LINES

One June day in 1921 a man called Alfred Watkins, a Herefordshire brewer and amateur archaeologist, was out riding his horse in his native county, when he experienced what he called *a flood of ancestral memory*. Looking at the familiar landscape, he suddenly saw it as never before, observing a pattern in the countryside of criss-cross straight lines which seemed to link churches, burial mounds, castles and cross-roads. He was convinced that he had experienced a *flashback* of the countryside as it was in the time of the Ancient Britons, with a network of paths, some of which were aligned to either a star or the sun. He called this network *Ley Lines*.

Other antiquarians began to investigate this phenomena and one known as Guy Underwood learnt dowsing in order to carry out his experiments. He discovered that all the churches and ancient sanctified sites were linked by the Ley Lines. He was of the opinion that both prehistoric and medieval builders were aware of these lines of force and had built sacred sites on them using some ancient law, attempting to harness the energies for beneficial means. There are many books written on this subject for anyone wishing to explore it further.

My belief is that present man has lost the knowledge and most of his inner feelings and instinct. Consequently he has driven his material world through the network of Ley Lines, causing disruption and disturbance to the earth's natural energies. Train lines, motorways, new housing estates, all have disturbed and unsettled these lines. I feel that when we get blackspots on motorways and other routes it could be all linked to cutting through this Ley Line network on the earth.

I know that certain housing estates have problems, so the question has to be asked, what have the builders and planners done, what have they disturbed and upset? There is no doubt modern man has a lot to answer for, and I quite honestly think that our progression is only on a material level and spiritually we have seriously regressed.

We must start using our natural intuition more. Most of us resist these feelings, but there is undoubtedly something awakening deep inside many people, for they are searching and wanting to know and understand the psychic part of themselves. This I am sure is to do with the new Age of Aquarius the age of enlightenment and love.

Let us consider further the development of 'blackspots and negative areas'. If these Ley Lines are streams of positive energy, what happens if one is bisected, disturbed or built on? Think of a stream of water. If a natural stream is blocked it will find a different route. If such a route cannot be found it will cause the area around it to be come bogged down and swampy, it will become stagnant and unhealthy. A stream of positive energy disturbed, would react in the same manner, possibly causing illness, bad temper and depression. Even relationships can become effected and accidents can happen. Animal illness can also occur; the list is endless.

It is said that an experienced dowser, with time and patience, can do something to restore the natural energies that have been disturbed. It requires the placing of an angle iron and stakes bound with copper into the ground, which has the effect of reversing the negative and positive energies. However I think it is far too late for correction in a great many areas, and who in the various government departments would listen to such a proposal? Perhaps at some point people will begin to take this question seriously and start doing something about it.

Many of our churches today are built on Ley Lines; this is because it has been the practice to rebuild churches on the old sites and many are built on former Pagan sites and earthworks, the Christian religion modifying them for their own needs. Castles which were built in strategic positions providing good views over the countryside for defence purposes were also built on the Ley Lines. There is no doubt that ancient peoples used the Lines to avail themselves of the magical energy which was running from church to church, pagan site to pagan site. This ability and knowledge is now lost or perhaps lying dormant until the time comes for us to rediscover the power lying beneath the surface of the earth. Will this too be a product of the new Aquarian Age? Simply by understanding the meaning of the term Ley Line we are acknowledging the existence of some kind of energy field; this is a start.

I believe that the great monuments of Stonehenge, the Rollright Stones, Avebury and others scattered across the country, are enormous energy centres which generate power at certain times of the year. I also feel that this energy is getting stronger and is helping to germinate the seed which is in every one of us, drawing us back to our roots, and the deep knowledge of the Pagans, Druids and others who worked with, rather than against the earth's natural rhythms.

The concept of natural earth energy is nothing new. All over the world this energy has been accepted and used by ancient tribes. The Sioux Indians for instance, used the Standing Rock in South Dakota. By standing up straight against the Rock they renewed their own energies and psychic powers. I myself experience this recharging when I visit Glastonbury and walk up the Tor, or sometimes when I visit the Rollright Stones.

If we can imagine the planet earth as a huge living body, with strong lines of energy, like arteries running through her, then we see how we have chopped and smothered her surface without any consideration for her health and well being, and without understanding how these energies could have helped us. We have instead created a very sick world. We must learn to heal our mother earth and undo all the harm that we have inflicted over the years.

I realise that many people will find it hard to accept my feelings on this, but I hope that it will open minds to just some aspects, and maybe as we discover more, we may receive untold wisdom which will throw most people's logic to the wind. We are indeed moving into an age where science is beginning to accept ideas about the universe that would have been looked upon with scorn by the scientists of yesteryear. My advice is to always keep an open mind.

UFOs OR NATURAL PHENOMENA?

This extract is from a letter sent to me by a couple who came to the talk I gave at Coventry on UFOs. They are Shirley and Chris Elliott of Balsall Common, Coventry; the date they witnessed the following was Thursday August 13th 1992 at approximately 11.10 pm (23.10 hrs).

"We had been visiting friends at Wolverton near Claverdon/Henley in Arden and on returning home we both suddenly noticed and shouted to each other "did you see that light in the sky?". In appearance, it was a large turquoise, blue/green sphere (rugby ball size) with a longish tail, shooting down from

the sky in front of us towards the earth in the direction we were travelling. It only appeared for what must have been seconds in time before disappearing. My wife and I did not really think much more about it, although we wondered what it might have been, but nothing had been printed in any of the local or national newspapers.

It was only when attending your talk on UFOs that I mentioned to you in passing what we had seen. From our description you showed us a picture from the UFO book which was exactly what we had seen and described to you, but was referred to as a fireball. My wife and I can now confirm a second sighting of a fireball which although the same in colour and appearance was in fact much smaller in size but seemed to disappear or 'burn out' in the sky, i.e. it did not seem to be heading downwards towards the earth, but across the sky. This second sighting was over Balsall Common. These details are as accurate, although brief, as my wife and I can confirm, bearing in mind we only saw them for a brief moment, i.e. seconds in time. They are however factual and are forwarded to you, the date and time of the second sighting was November 16th approximately 10.30 pm (22.30 hrs).'

There are numerous sightings all over the world, some recorded some not, and a great many people do not say anything in case they are made to look silly, or they sometimes do not know who to report the sighting to.

It is surprising how many people have these experiences and I do feel now that people are beginning to discuss what they have seen, because it is becoming more acceptable to talk about such matters. Programmes are being made on the subject both on radio and television, and reports can be seen in the national papers.

Just recently, residents in Hartcliffe, Bristol witnessed eight different lights changing from blue to red, and the sighting continued until 5.30 am. It appears Bristol Airport Chiefs and weather experts were baffled by the mystery.

I anticipate writing more on the subject of UFOs at a later date.

CONCLUSION

My aim as in the first book, has been to encourage readers to develop an open-minded approach to all matters spiritual. Without this, there can be no progress in individual development.

When writing, I intended to provide my *Thoughts On The Way* that would stimulate further development, but as before, I must stress that I believe further progress has to be supported by extensive reading of the available literature.

Our individual personal attitude towards our fellow human beings, towards animals, our consideration for all living matter and especially for our planet, should reveal the utmost respect and care. For some, adopting such a stance could be the first step along the pathway.

My other plea is for those truly interested in developing awareness and spirituality, to try to meet others who are treading the same footpath. During the last few years, groups of like-minded people have sprung up in many towns and cities and offer a variety of topics, guest speakers and discussion groups. Go to as many as possible and only then will it become evident which is your particular route for development, but as always be open-minded throughout.

Good luck in your quest!

GLOSSARY

Akashic records
They are to be found on the astral plane, and are a historical record of everything that has and will occur. Some mediums have access to these records.

Astral level
The realm entered by the spiritual part of man after death, and the dwelling of higher spiritual bodies. It is invisible, and yet can be entered in a sleep state or in a state of altered consciousness.

Aura
An energy field surrounding the human body showing colours which differ according to each individual. Many psychics are able to see the aura and its colour.

Clairvoyance
This means clearseeing and is the ability to receive information by seeing mentally that which exists out of normal sight.

Great White Brotherhood
A group which has attained high spiritual perfection, and which includes masters such as Jesus and the Lord Buddha.

Karma
The law of cause and effect; it could be seen as the law of consequences when the fruits of action in one lifetime determine the conditions of life in the next.

Medium
A person who has the ability to communicate with the spirit world.

Ouija board
Ouija is derived from the French and German words for yes. It was originally designed as a board game, but is now used as a means of communicating with spirits. It is dangerous and should not be used without the presence of a trained medium.

Paranormal
Events which lie beyond normal scientific investigation.

Psychometry
A method of sensing or reading from physical objects, the history of each object and matters and people associated.

Trance Medium
A medium who communicates in a state of trance with spirit.

UFOs
Unidentified flying objects.